Instructional Book

Chris Kiana Sr., MBA, MA

ORIGINAL
100
Alaska ESKIMO YO-YO
STRATAGEMS

Instructional Book

Chris Kiana Sr., MBA, MA

Since 1978

PO Box 221974 Anchorage, Alaska 99522-1974

ISBN 1-59433-013-1

Library of Congress Catalog Card Number: 2004092180

Manufactured in the United States of America

Dedication

Dedicated to my mother, Minnie Kiana Morken, who passed away in 2004.

Contents

Legend:
VEO=Vertical Eskimo Orbit;
HEO=Horizontal Eskimo Orbit;
OEO=Overhead Eskimo Orbit

Acknowledgments

I express grattitude to my Inupiaq Eskimo grandmother and grandfather, who taught me how to operate the Eskimo Yo-Yo at age three.

.

History of Eskimo Yo-Yo
Revolving from Bolo Weapon

All civilizations at probably had a form of the bolo weapon, which was used as a weapon by Australians to engage the enemy and harvest game in Australia such as the kangaroo and Eskimos harvested game in Alaska such as waterfowl, grouse, ptarmigan, and rabbits.

I have talked to my Native Elders, including our oldest Inupiaq Eskimo Elders for the name bolo weapon or Eskimo Yo-Yo. One can only guess that early explorers who visited Alaska before and after the turn of the last century, they saw an Eskimo spinning the stringed cultural artifact and simply named it Eskimo Yo-Yo.

Historically and culturally, we were raised and taught our Inupiaq Eskimo traditional ways of learning and being taught by our Native Elders the ongoing processes necessary to keep our tribes intact though tradition, culture, storytelling, and the hunting and fishing processes. This was necessary for us to stay alive, which we have done for centuries in what is now called Alaska.

Our Inupiaq Eskimo girls were taught how to sew, cook, put up our camps, and bear children while the boys were taught how to become traditional hunters every harvesting season of the year. Through this learning process, our ancestors were taught how to stay in shape and have the stamina necessary for every hunter to have for the food-gathering.

The young Eskimo boys were taught how to use the bolo weapon, spear, bow and arrow, club and knives, which were our earliest and shistoical weapons. We were taught how to use them effectively as weapons and for the food-gathering process, which was an almost every day process.

From the bolo weapon, the Eskimo Yo-Yo probably emerged. By using the Eskimo Yo-Yo toy, we learned the manual dexterity of using our hands and arms better.

At this present time in our history, Native American now use the modern weapons such as the rifle and pistol to hunt game with and utilize transportation such as the ATV, river and sea boats, and the airplane.

The Eskimo Yo-Yo probably stayed in our cultures today because of being sewn from leftover fur scraps that fur hats, mukluks (fur boots), gloves, and other sewn items. The 1,000,000 tourists that annually come to Alaska favor taking home a unique Eskimo Yo-Yo to hang up as a wall decoration because they often look ornamental.

The main reason that Eskimo Yo-Yos are still alive in our Inupiaq Eskimo Culture is probably definitely because of the tourist trade. I know of one store in Anchorage that sells six 50 gallon barrels of Eskimo Yo-Yos alone during the tourist season that starts in April and ends in September of every year.

Disclaimer

P ublication Consultants or the author and inventor, Chris Kiana Sr. will not be responsible for injuries due to unsafe handling on its operations due to the following conditions.

The Eskimo Yo-Yo has been operated for thousands of years safely since being developed from the bolo weapon.

Safety Procedures for Operation the Eskimo Yo-Yo

•It is strongly recommended for everyone operating the toy in a safe manner at all times and not use it like a bolo weapon or in a reckless manner.

•It is also recommend that safety glasses be worn when operating the Eskimo Yo-Yo or a toy-like form of it.

•One must always operate the toy in an open and safe area and especially, not near anyone.

•The operator should avoid having the twirling objects/orbiters from hitting anyone and themselves.

•Do not twirl the orbiters fast, but just fast enough to operate them in a safe manner.

•If you find yourself operating the Eskimo Yo-Yo/toy out of control or unsafe manner, immediately stop the twirling and start again.

•Always check the string, orbiters and handle, insuring it is safe to operate in a safe manner.

Conclusion

It is the author's goal to successfully introduce this cultural artifact/toy to you so you may have the opportunity to meet the challenge of being able to operate the Eskimo Yo-Yo or toy. This is what life is all about, satisfying our curiosity and to see if we have the ability to master the operations of the Eskimo Yo-Yo.

I do not guarantee that you will not be able to perform these tricks/ stratagems, as I have found out some people can't do certain things in life they try to accomplish. Take for instance, I can't operate the hackie sac, which has been a moderately success toy for the past decade. I can only kick the hackie sac, maybe twice.

I simply want to share this with the world. Good luck on the operations of the Eskimo Yo-Yo or toy.

Additional Information about the Eskimo Yo-Yo

You will have a higher degree of confidence in yourself and abilities once you have learned to master the wide variety of tricks, feats, or stratagems necessary to accomplish the multitude of operations on the Alaska Eskimo Yo-Yo. You will note the quantity of tricks listed in the Table of Contents will revert back to one of three major stratagems: Vertical Eskimo Orbit, Horizontal Eskimo Orbit, or Overhead Eskimo Orbit.

At first glance, you will think the operations of the cultural artifact look simple to operate. However, once you start learning them, you may start thinking differently. From time to time, the stratagems are even difficult to operate for me. I sometimes forget the unique motions needed to do the different operations of the Eskimo Yo-Yo. You will revert back to one of the three or a combination of feats consisting of: Vertical Eskimo Orbit; Horizontal Eskimo Orbit; and Overhead Eskimo Orbit.

I have been told the operations of the Eskimo Yo-Yo become repetitious after awhile as one starts to learn a number of the tricks. This is quite the contrary. The end results may be the same, but it is following through and performing the first stages of the stratagems that it different from other tricks.

The Eskimo Yo-Yo has been overlooked this past century during the settlement of Alaska, which probably was also hampered because of Eskimos not having a written language until the 1950s. Until then, our Eskimo history was passed down for centuries by world of mouth.

I remember selling newspapers at Fairbanks, Alaska and reading the historical article about our word of mouth passed down Inupiaq Eskimo history being transformed into a written language. The University of Alaska at Fairbanks in the 1950s obtained a grant to construct and write Eskimo words. Now we have a written history.

Finally, I saw the potential of what I call a sleeper that has been overlooked this past century. I have taken the time to invent the stratagems and write the tricks. It is my life goal to world fad the Eskimo Yo-Yo or find a toy company to make a prototype, and successfully market it nationally and internationally.

At this time, I am the best operator in the world out of six billion plus people who can operate all the tricks or stratagems. However, I am anxiously waiting for people to learn the 100 stratagems so I may have the opportunity to teach everyone the second 100 Eskimo Yo-Yo tricks. This is the most simple, yet most complex cultural artifact/toy in the world today.

Chris Kiana's Personal History and Belief of working with the Eskimo Yo-Yo

I grew up with the Eskimo Yo-Yo in my back pocket and naturally twirled it everywhere I went. The cultural artifact just seemed to be a part of me and I took it for granted that it had to be with me always. As I reached my teen years, I lost slight interest in the Eskimo Yo-Yo. While I was in the service in 1968, I had mom sew me a dozen yo-yos and I put on a yo-yo exhibition at the YMCA Navy and Marines Christmas Party in San Diego. I kept almost 500 military personal busy for an hour of the show. I was satisfied that I had done a good deed at the time.

During this time, the click-clackers faded across the nation and I knew the Eskimo Yo-Yo could also fad, if marketed correctly, but it wasn't to be. An attempt was made in the 1990s by a catalog ordering company, but it was advertised in a catalog, but was meant to be a show and tell toy, to be sold on TV commercials or where there were large on-going numbers of people. I proved this by market testing it to 100,000 people traffic for four weeks at a shopping mall, selling 1,250 of them. By doing this, I knew there was a market for the toy.

Now, I know that my timing is right for a second edition of the instructional book.

Chronological History of
Working with the Eskimo Yo-Yo

1946   Taught how to operate the Eskimo Yo-Yo at age three by my Inupiaq Eskimo grandmother and grandfather.

1946 - 1979 - Learned and invented a dozen tricks

1968   Knew there would be a market for yo-yo due to Click-Clackers fad on the world toy market.

1979   Found out there weren't any written instructions on yo-yo

1980   Started inventing and writing tricks on Eskimo Yo-Yo

1985   Published 50 instructional book and performed market test on yo-yo.

1987   Invented and wrote 100 instructional tricks on the Eskimo Yo-Yo.

1988   Completed 40 instructional professional minutes of yo-yo video.

1989 - 1990 Started looking for toy company to produce Eskimo Yo-Yo Toy.

1992   authored First Edition of 100 trick Book.

1992   Found a toy company who took on Eskimo Yo-Yo toy.

1993   Debut of Orbitron toy at NYC Toy Fair Show.

1993 – 1994 Approximately 50,000 Orbitrons sold.

1994   Invented 30 rubber ball ultra-expert trick of Eskimo Yo-Yo.

1995   Toy company took Orbitron off market.

1995 – 2004 Looking for another toy company take over Eskimo Yo-Yo toy.

2004 Doing second edition of 100 trick book.

Alaska Eskimo Yo-Yo

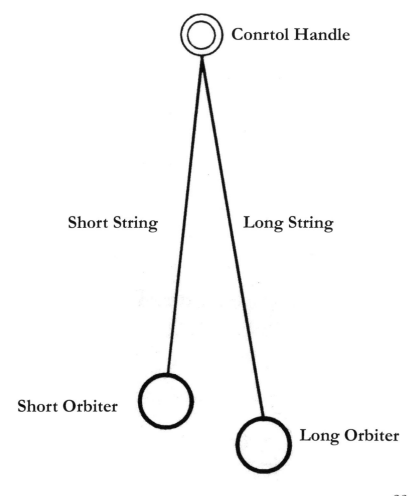

Conrtol Handle

Short String

Long String

Short Orbiter

Long Orbiter

1. Vertical Eskimo Orbit

A. Hold Eskimo Yo-Yo as shown.

B. Twirl longer orbiter in clockwise vertical movement.

C. Toss shorter orbiter in opposite direction when longer orbiter is to operator's left side.

D. Achieve Vertical Eskimo Orbit.

2. Horizontal Eskimo Orbit

A. Hold Eskimo Yo-Yo
as shown.

B. Twirl longer orbiter
in clockwise horizontal
movement.

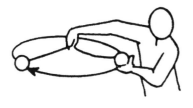

C. Toss shorter orbiter
in opposite direction
when longer orbiter is
across from operator.

D Achieve Horizontal
Eskimo Orbit

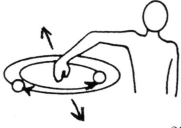

3. Overhead Eskimo Orbit

A. Hold Eskimo Yo-Yo as shown.

B. Twirl longer orbiter overhead in clockwise direction.

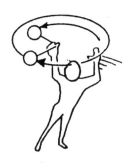

C. Toss shorter orbiter in opposite direction when longer orbiter is across from operator.

D. Achieve Overhead Eskimo Orbit.

4. Single Floor Pickup
Vertical Eskimo Orbit

A. Place Eskimo Yo-Yo
on floor as shown.

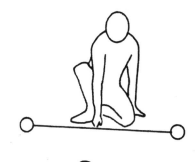

B. Stand up quickly
and start short vertical
movements of Eskimo
Yo-Yo.

C. Achieve Vertical
Eskimo Orbit.

5. Loop the Foot Start
Vertical Eskimo Orbit

A. Sit on a chair, extend your leg out and loop Eskimo Yo-Yo over your foot as shown.

B Raise Eskimo Yo-Yo quickly in upward direction causing orbiters to hit your foot.

C. Achieve Vertical Eskimo Orbit.

6. Loop the Knee Start
Vertical Eskimo Orbit

A. Place foot on bottom step and place Eskimo Yo-Yo over knee as shown.

C. Raise Eskimo Yo-Yo quickly in upward direction causing orbiters to hit your leg.

D. Achieve Vertical Eskimo Orbit.

7. Half Table Start
Vertical Eskimo Orbit

A. Place longer orbiter on tabletop as shown.

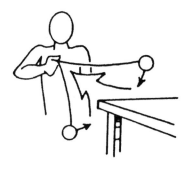

B. Grasp handle and pull upward in 45-degree direction.

C. Achieve Vertical Eskimo Orbit.

8. Pendulum Start
Vertical Eskimo Orbit

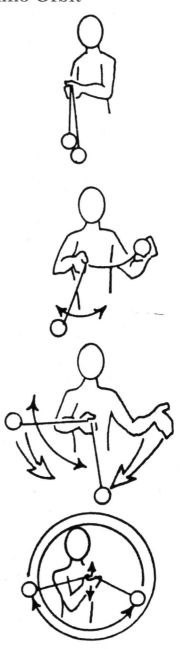

A. Allow longer orbiter hang down and hold Eskimo Yo-Yo as shown.

B. Start rocking longer orbiter back and forth as shown.

C. When longer orbiter is opposite of held orbiter, drop shorter orbiter down.

D. Achieve Vertical Eskimo Orbit.

9. Half Pendulum Start
Vertical Eskimo Orbit

A. Hold Eskimo Yo-Yo as shown.

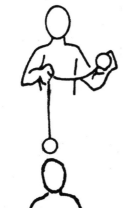

B. Hold shorter orbiter as shown.

C. Drop shorter orbiter allowing it to fall downward.

D. Achieve Vertical Eskimo Orbit.

10. Hand Switch
Vertical Eskimo Orbit

A. Achieve Vertical
Eskimo Orbit.

B. Switch operating
hand continuing Vertical
Eskimo Orbit.

C. Switch back to
original hand continuing
Vertical Eskimo Orbit.

11. Hand Switch
Horizontal Eskimo Orbit

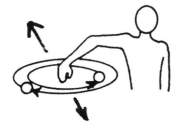

A. Achieve Horizontal Eskimo Orbit.

B. Switch operating hand continuing Horizontal Eskimo Orbit.

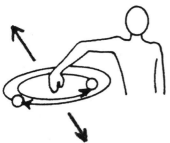

C. Switch back to original hand continuing Horizontal Eskimo Orbit.

12. Help Start
Vertical Eskimo Orbit

A. Have friend hold
Eskimo Yo-Yo as
shown.

B. Friend tosses orbiters
upward with both
hands.

C. Achieve Vertical
Eskimo Orbit.

13. Jack Knife
Vertical Eskimo Orbit

A. Achieve Vertical Eskimo Orbit.

B. Switch operating hand from short vertical movements to horizontal movements.

C. Achieve Vertical Eskimo Orbit.

14. Jack Knife — Switch Hands
Vertical Eskimo Orbit

A. Achieve Vertical
Eskimo Orbit.

B. Switch from doing
vertical movements to
horizontal operating
movements.

C. Switch back to
vertical operating
movements.

D. Switch back to
horizontal operating
movements.

15. Jack Knife
Horizontal Eskimo Orbit

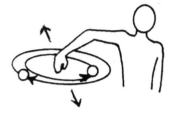

A. Achieve Horizontal Eskimo Orbit

B. Switch from front and back movements to sideways operating movement.

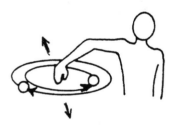

C. Switch back to front and back operating movements.

16. Twirl Around Fist Start
Vertical Eskimo Orbit

A. Hold Eskimo Yo-Yo
as shown.

B. Twirl orbiters around
striking hand.

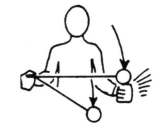

C. Quickly jerk up on
hand causing orbiter to
go upward.

D. Achieve Vertical Eskimo
Orbit.

17. Self Help — Loop The Chair Legs Horizontal Eskimo Orbit

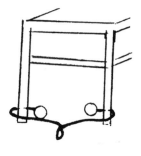

A. Place Eskimo Yo-Yo on floor as shown.

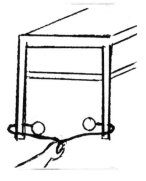

B. Grasp handle and stand up at the same time.

C. Start horizontal operating movements of Eskimo Yo-Yo.

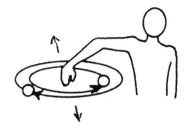

D. Achieve Horizontal Eskimo Orbit.

18. Self Start — Loop One Chair Leg Horizontal Eskimo Orbit

A. Place Eskimo Yo-Yo on floor as shown.

B. Grasp handle and stand up at the same time.

C. Start horizontal operating movements of Eskimo Yo-Yo.

D. Achieve Horizontal Eskimo Orbit.

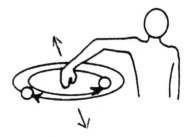

19. Pull One Orbiter Off Shoulder Start Vertical Eskimo Orbit

A. Place Eskimo Yo-Yo on shoulder as shown.

B. Grasp handle of Eskimo Yo-Yo.

C. Pull outward away from you causing orbiter to flip over your shoulder.

D. Achieve Vertical Eskimo Orbit.

20. Pull Both Orbiters Over Each Shoulder
Start—Vertical Eskimo Orbit

A. Put orbiters over
each should as shown.

B. Grasp handle of
Eskimo Yo-Yo.

C. Pull handle away
from you causing
orbiters to over
shoulders.

D. Achieve Vertical
Eskimo Orbit.

21. Drop One Orbiter Off Tabletop Vertical Eskimo Orbit

A. Place Eskimo Yo-Yo as shown.

B. Allow longer orbiter to swing downwards and start vertical movement of handle.

C. Achieve Vertical Eskimo Orbit.

D. Start vertical movements and achieve Vertical Eskimo Orbit.

22. Drop Orbiters Off Table Tabletop Vertical Eskimo Orbit

A. Place Eskimo Yo-Yo as shown.

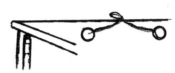

B. Grasp handle and pull upward slowly at a 45-degree angle away from table.

C. Lower operating arm, allowing both orbiters to swing downwards.

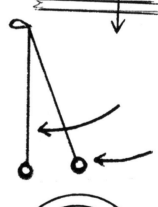

D. Start vertical movements and achieve Vertical Eskimo Orbit.

23. Drop Both Orbiters Off Tabletop Horizontal Eskimo Orbit

A. Place Eskimo Yo-Yo on tabletop as shown.

B. Grasp handle and quickly or slowly pull Eskimo Yo-Yo away from table.

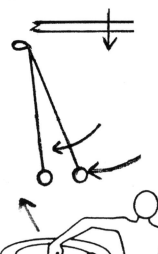

C. Allow orbiters to leave table and start horizontal movements.

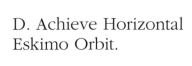

D. Achieve Horizontal Eskimo Orbit.

24. Under The Table Toss Start
Vertical Eskimo Orbit

A. Hold Eskimo Yo-Yo
as shown.

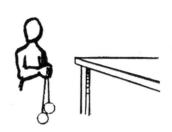

B. Rock orbiters back
and forth until you have
enough force to swing
them toward beneath
the table top edge.

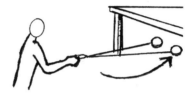

C. Allow longer orbiter
to hit under tabletop
and allow shorter
orbiter to swing around.

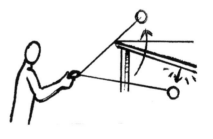

D. Achieve Vertical
Eskimo Orbit.

25. Loop The Chair Leg
Horizontal Eskimo Orbit

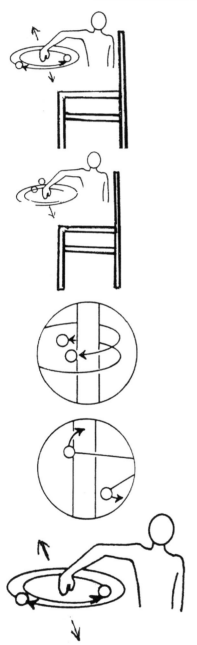

A. Stand three feet away from corner of a chair leg while achieving Horizontal Eskimo Orbit.

B. Take a slight step forward when orbiters are behind you.

C. Allow orbiters to swing around chair let.

D. Pull slightly, allowing orbiter to come back around.

E. Step back and achieve Horizontal Eskimo Orbit.

26. Kick Start
Vertical Eskimo Orbit

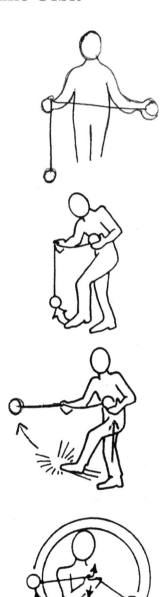

A. Hold Eskimo Yo-Yo
as shown.

B. Lift leg up quickly
toward longer orbiter.

C. Kick orbiter allowing
it to swing upward
to 9 o'clock position
and toss held orbiter
upward.

D. Achieve Vertical
Eskimo Orbit.

27. Kick Start
Horizontal Eskimo Orbit

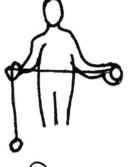

A. Hold Eskimo Yo-Yo as shown.

B. Lift leg up quickly toward longer orbiter.

C. Kick orbiter lightly to bring it up to 9 o'clock position and toss held orbiter upward.

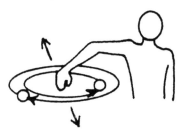

D. Achieve Horizontal Eskimo Orbit.

28. Overhead Door Start
Vertical Eskimo Orbit

A. Hold Eskimo Yo-Yo and under doorway as shown.

B. Rock orbiters to one side and swing with enough force to bring orbiters upward.

C. Allow longer orbiter to hit door causing it to go in opposite direction.

D. Achieve Vertical Eskimo Orbit.

29. Around The World
Horizontal Eskimo Orbit

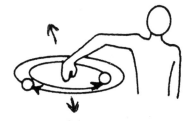

A. Achieve Horizontal Eskimo Orbit.

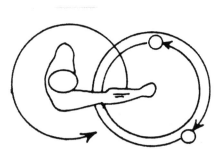

B. Turn slowly around in a circle while achieving Horizontal Eskimo Orbit.

30. Around The World
Overhead Eskimo Orbit

A. Achieve Overhead
Eskimo Orbit.

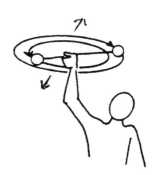

B. Turn slowly around
in a full circle while
achieving Overhead
Eskimo Orbit.

31. Loop Orbiter Over Chair
Vertical Eskimo Orbit

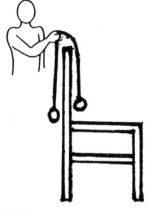

A. Hold Eskimo Yo-Yo over back of chair as shown.

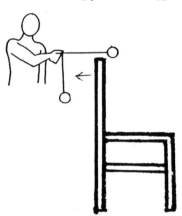

B. Pull Eskimo Yo-Yo fast enough away from back of chair causing orbiter to hit it and go upward.

C. Achieve Vertical Eskimo Orbit.

32. Dead Start
Vertical Eskimo Orbit

A. Hold Eskimo Yo-Yo
as shown.

B. Start short vertical
movements causing
orbiters to swing back
and forth.

C. Achieve Vertical
Eskimo Orbit

33. Dead Start
Horizontal Eskimo Orbit

A. Hold Eskimo Yo-Yo as shown.

B. Start front and back horizontal movements with operating arm.

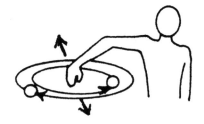

C. Achieve Horizontal Eskimo Orbit.

34. Twirl Around Start
Horizontal Eskimo Orbit

A. Hold orbiter in one
hand as shown.

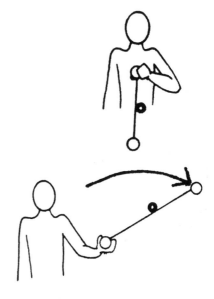

B. Twirl Eskimo Yo-Yo
around in clockwise
position and release
orbiter.

C. Catch handle of
Eskimo Yo-Yo and start
horizontal movements.

D. Achieve Horizontal
Eskimo Orbit.

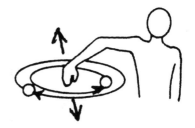

35. Belt Horizontal Start
Horizontal Eskimo Orbit

A. Hold orbiters around your waist as shown or have some one hold them.

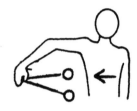

B. Release orbiters and quickly pull away from your waist.

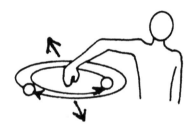

C. Achieve Horizontal Eskimo Orbit.

36. Belt Horizontal Start
Vertical Eskimo Orbit

A. Hold orbiters around your waist or have someone hold them.

B. Release orbiters and slowly pull away from your waist.

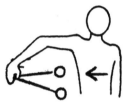

C. Start vertical movement and achieve Vertical Eskimo Orbit.

37. Twirl Around Start
Vertical Eskimo Orbit

A. Hold orbiter of Eskimo Yo-Yo as shown.

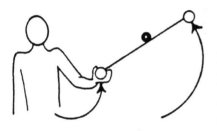

B. Rock and twirl held orbiter around in counterclockwise direction.

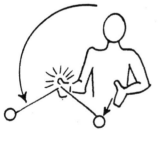

C. Catch handle of Eskimo Yo-Yo as it is twirled around.

D. Start vertical movements and achieve Vertical Eskimo Orbit.

38. Twirl Around Foot Start
Vertical Eskimo Orbit

A. Sit on chair of bottom stem holding Eskimo Yo-Yo as shown.

B. Rock and twirl Eskimo Yo-Yo around in counter-clock position.

C. Allow longer orbiter to hit extended foot allowing shorter orbiter to swing around.

D. Start vertical movements and achieve Vertical Eskimo Orbit.

39. Table Pickup Start
Horizontal Eskimo Orbit

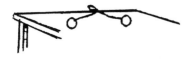

A. Place Eskimo Yo-Yo on tabletop as shown.

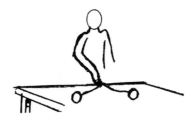

B. Grasp handle of Eskimo Yo-Yo.

C. Quickly pull Eskimo Yo-Yo away from tabletop.

D. Achieve Horizontal Eskimo Orbit.

40. Reverse Pickup Table Start
Horizontal Eskimo Orbit

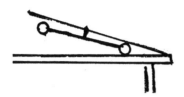

A. Place Eskimo Yo-Yo
on tabletop as shown.

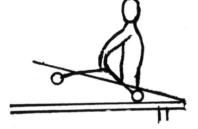

B. Face away from table
and grasp handle.

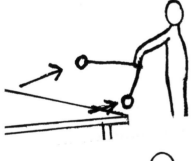

C. Quickly pull Eskimo
Yo-Yo away from
tabletop.

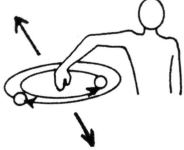

D. Start horizontal
movements and achieve
Horizontal Eskimo
Orbit.

63

41. Toss Start
Vertical Eskimo Orbit

A. Hold orbiter of Eskimo Yo-Yo as shown.

B. Rock back and forth until you twirl Eskimo Yo-Yo upward, releasing held orbiter and cause it to twirl in circles above you.

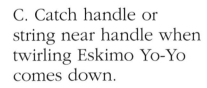

C. Catch handle or string near handle when twirling Eskimo Yo-Yo comes down.

D. Start vertical movements and achieve Vertical Eskimo Orbit.

42. Toss Start
Horizontal Eskimo Orbit

A. Hold orbiter of
Eskimo Yo-Yo as
shown.

C. Rock back and forth
until you twirl Eskimo
Yo-Yo upward, releasing
held orbiter and cause it
to twirl in circles above
you.

C. Catch handle or
string near handle when
twirling Eskimo Yo-Yo
comes down.

D. Start horizontal
movements and achieve
Horizontal Eskimo
Orbit.

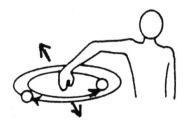

43. Overhead Tabletop Start
Overhead Eskimo Orbit

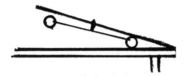

A. Place Eskimo Yo-Yo on tabletop as shown.

B. Kneel down close to tabletop and grasp Eskimo Yo-Yo.

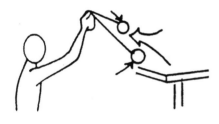

C. Pull on handle upward in a 45-degree angle and stand up at the same time.

D. Achieve Overhead Eskimo Orbit.

44. Loop The Wrist Start — Flip Vertical Eskimo Orbit

A. Place Eskimo Yo-Yo over both wrists as shown.

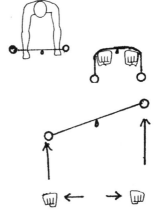

B. Jerk wrists outward from each other causing Eskimo Yo-Yo to twirls upward.

C. Allow twirling Eskimo Yo-Yo to come down and catch handle or string near handle.

D. Catch handle or string near handle.

E. Start vertical movements and achieve Vertical Eskimo Orbit.

45. Horizontal Eskimo Orbit — Loop The Chair Legs Reverse Directions — Horizontal Eskimo Orbit

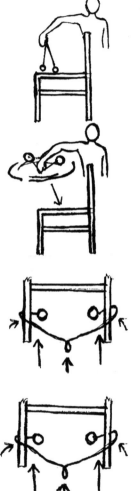

A. Hold held Eskimo Yo-Yo standing broadside to chair legs.

B. Achieve Horizontal Eskimo Orbit, stoop down, allow both orbiters to swing behind you and move operating arm toward the middle area of chair legs.

C. Allow both orbiters to loop around, one on each chair leg.

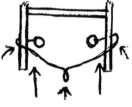

D. Jerk back slightly on handle allowing orbiters to swing back around.

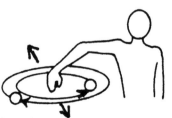

E. Start horizontal movements and achieve Horizontal Eskimo Orbit.

46. Behind The Back — Loop The Foot
Reverse Directions — Vertical Eskimo Orbit

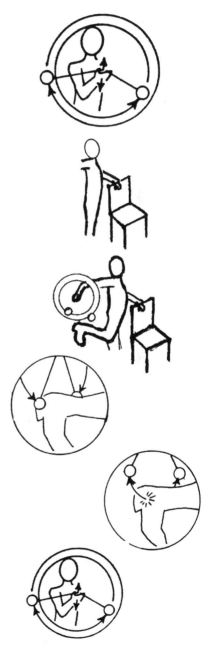

A. Achieve Vertical Eskimo orbit.

B. Turn around and put hand on chair back for support.

C. Raise leg while continuing to achieve Vertical Eskimo Orbit.

D. Lower operating arm when both orbiters reach 12 o'clock position and lower operating arm, allowing orbiters to swing around toward shoe.

E. Allow both swinging orbiters to hit shoe and continue short vertical movements.

F. Achieve Vertical Eskimo Orbit.

47. Loop Foot — Reverse Directions Vertical Eskimo Orbit

A. Achieve Vertical Eskimo Orbit.

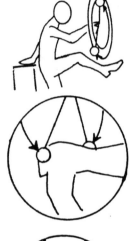

B. Put hand solid object for support and raise let toward twirling orbiters.

C. Allow orbiters to swing toward extended foot.

D. Allow both orbiters to hit shoe and continue vertical movements of Eskimo Yo-Yo.

E. Achieve Vertical Eskimo Orbit.

48. Vertical Eskimo Orbit — Flip — 360 Vertical Eskimo Orbit

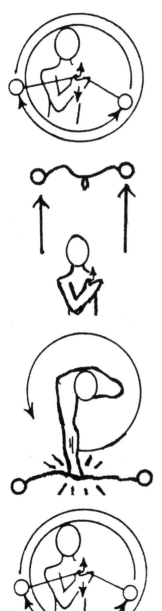

A. Achieve Vertical Eskimo Orbit

B. When both orbiters reach 6 o'clock position, flip and release held handle upward.

C. Turn in a complete circle while Eskimo Yo-Yo is twirling upward, then downwards in the air, and catching it when you have moved in a complete circle.

D. Achieve Vertical Eskimo Orbit.

49. Twirl Around Wrist — Flip
Vertical Eskimo Orbit

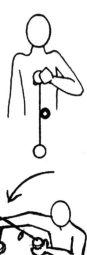

A. Hold one orbiter of Eskimo Yo-Yo as show.

B. Rock back and forth, twirling around counterclockwise until it loops arm.

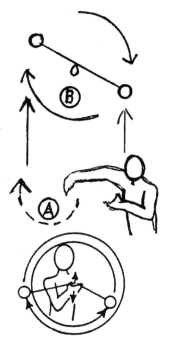

C. Release held orbiter, allowing it to twirl around in clockwise direction, jerking arm slightly to flip Eskimo Yo-Yo in a circling pattern and wait for it to come back down.

D. Grab handle or string near handle, do vertical movements, and achieve Vertical Eskimo Orbit.

50. Loop Wrist Start With A Partner Vertical Eskimo Orbit

A. Place Eskimo Yo-Yo on a volunteer's wrist as shown.

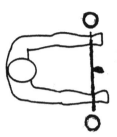

B. Grasp handle and pull upward causing orbiters to hit volunteer's wrist and go in opposite directions.

C. Start vertical movements and achieve Vertical Eskimo Orbit.

51. Loop Chair Seat Start Vertical Eskimo Orbit

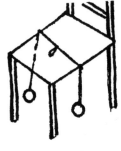

A. Put Eskimo Yo-Yo on chair seat as shown.

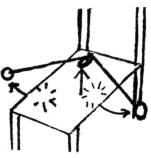

B. Pull up handle of Eskimo Yo-Yo slightly causing orbiters to hit each side of chair and go in opposite directions.

C. Achieve Vertical Eskimo Orbit.

52. Horizontal Dead Start
Horizontal Eskimo Orbit

A. Hold Eskimo Yo-Yo
as shown.

B. Start short horizontal
movements back and
forth to your side.

C. Achieve Horizontal
Eskimo Orbit.

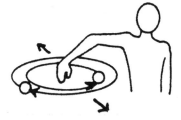

53. Vertical Toss — Loop Fingers Vertical Eskimo Orbit

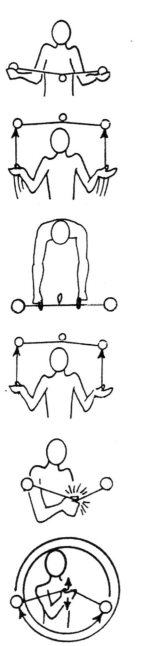

A. Hold Orbiters in each hand as shown.

B. Toss both orbiters upward into air.

C. Allow orbiters to loop index finger on each hand when it comes back down.

D. Flip left index finger outward and right finger upward causing Eskimo Yo-Yo to flip into air in circular motion.

E. Catch handle or string near handle and start short vertical movements.

F. Achieve Vertical Eskimo Orbit.

54. Dead Start — Vertical Toss
Vertical Eskimo Orbit

A. Hold Eskimo Yo-Yo
as shown.

B. Quickly toss Eskimo
Yo-Yo into air allowing
it to several feet into the
air.

C. Catch handle or
string near handle
and start vertical
movements.

D. Achieve Vertical
Eskimo Orbit.

55. Over And Under — Overhead, Vertical, and Horizontal Eskimo Orbits

A. Achieve Overhead Eskimo Orbit.

B. Slowly start downwards until at Vertical Eskimo Orbit.

C. Slowly start downwards until at Horizontal Eskimo Orbits.

D. Slowly continue operation upward until you are at Overhead Eskimo Orbit.

56. Loop Chair Leg
One Orbiter — Horizontal Eskimo Orbits

A. Place Eskimo Yo-Yo
on floor as shown.

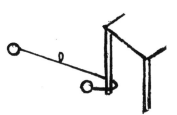

B. Kneel down to pick
up handle of Eskimo
Yo-Yo.

C. Stand up quickly
and start back and front
hand movements.

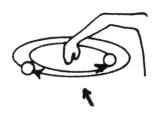

D. Achieve Horizontal
Eskimo Orbit.

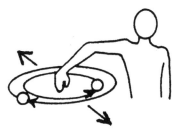

57. Vertical Eskimo Orbit — Flip Vertical Eskimo Orbit

A. Achieve Vertical Eskimo Orbit.

B. When orbiters reach 6 o'clock position, flip Eskimo Yo-Yo into air several feet.

C. Catch Handle or string near handle

D. Achieve Vertical Eskimo Orbit.

58. Loop The Fingers — Flip Vertical Eskimo Orbit

A. Place Eskimo Yo-Yo on index fingers as shown.

B. Jerk outward with hands causing Eskimo Yo-Yo to go into air.

C. Catch handle or string near handle and start vertical movements.

D. Achieve Vertical Eskimo Orbit.

59. Overhead Eskimo Orbit — Hand Switch — Overhead Eskimo Orbit

A. Achieve Overhead Eskimo Orbit.

B. Switch operating hands.

C. Switch operating hands and continue Overhead Eskimo Orbit.

60. Full Conversion — Horizontal, Vertical, and Overhead Eskimo Orbits

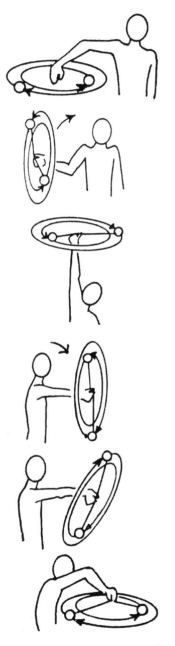

A. Achieve Horizontal Eskimo Orbit.

B. Start bringing up operating hand slowly.

C. Achieve Overhead Eskimo Orbit.

D. Slowly bring operating arm down to achieve Vertical Eskimo Orbit.

E. Start bringing operating arm down slowly.

F. Achieve Horizontal Eskimo Orbit.

61. Drop Orbiters Off Table Start Horizontal Eskimo Orbit

A. Place Eskimo Yo-Yo on tabletop as shown.

B. Grasp handle of Eskimo Yo-Yo.

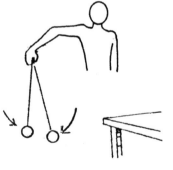

C. Pull on handle slowly allowing orbiters to fall off edge of table.

D. Start horizontal movements and achieve Horizontal Eskimo Orbit.

62. Friend — Help Toss Start
Vertical Eskimo Orbit

A. Friend stands several feet away from operator holding Eskimo Yo-Yo as shown.

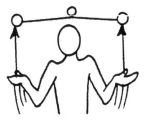

B. Friend tosses Eskimo Yo-Yo upward into air toward you.

C. You catch the handle or string near handle.

D. Start vertical movements and achieve Vertical Eskimo Orbit.

63. Friend — Help Toss Start — 360 Vertical Eskimo Orbit

A. Friend stands several feet away from operator holding Eskimo Yo-Yo as shown.

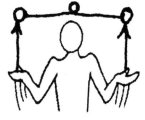

B. Friend tosses Eskimo Yo-Yo upward into air toward you.

C. You turn in a complete circle while tossed Eskimo Yo-Yo is in air.

D. You catch the handle or string near handle.

E. Achieve Vertical Eskimo Orbit.

64. Friend — Help Toss Start
Horizontal Eskimo Orbit

A. Friend stands several feet away from operator holding Eskimo Yo-Yo as shown.

B. Friend tosses Eskimo Yo-Yo upward into air toward you.

C. You catch the handle or string near handle

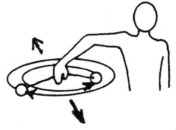

D. Start short horizontal movements and achieve Horizontal Eskimo Orbit.

65. Friend — Help Toss Start
360 Horizontal Eskimo Orbit

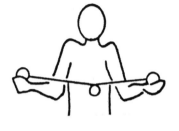

A. Friend stands several feet away from operator holding Eskimo Yo-Yo as shown.

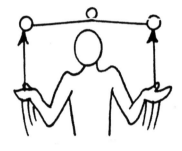

B. Friend tosses Eskimo Yo-Yo upward into air toward you.

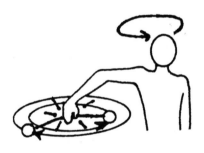

C. You turn in a complete circle while tossed Eskimo Yo-Yo is in air.

D. Catch the handle or string near handle and start horizontal movements and achieve Horizontal Eskimo Orbit.

66. Foot Flip
Vertical Eskimo Orbit

A. Sit on chair and cross leg over the other as shown.

B. Put Eskimo Yo-Yo orbiters on foot.

C. Quickly raise foot into air causing Eskimo Yo-Yo to go upward at least five feet.

D. Catch handle or string near handle and start vertical movements.

E. Achieve Vertical Eskimo Yo-Yo.

67. Horizontal Chair Legs Toss
Horizontal Eskimo Orbit

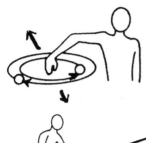

A. Operator Achieves Horizontal Eskimo Orbit.

B. Stoop over about three feet facing chair legs.

C. When both orbiters are behind you, toss and release Eskimo Yo-Yo toward chair legs.

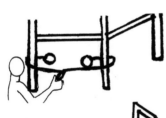

D. Quick grab handle or string near handle.

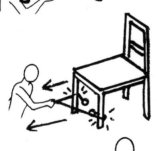

E. Pull slightly backwards on handle and make horizontal movements.

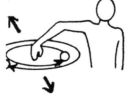

F. Stand up and achieve Horizontal Eskimo Orbit.

68. Horizontal Toss Loop Wrist Horizontal Eskimo Orbit

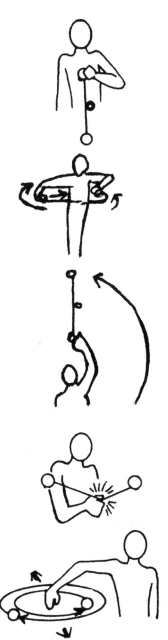

A. Hold Eskimo Yo-Yo as shown.

B. Twirl Eskimo Yo-Yo around yourself in clockwise direction.

C. Next, grab orbiter and swing it around clockwise.

D. Catch handle or string near handle and start vertical movements.

E. Bend arm and achieve Horizontal Eskimo Orbit.

69. Horizontal Toss — Loop Wrist — Flip Horizontal Eskimo Orbit

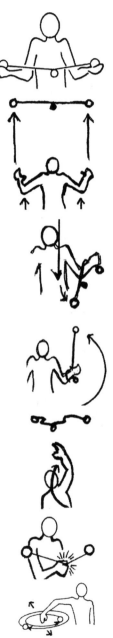

A. Hold Eskimo Yo-Yo as shown.

B. Toss held orbiters upward at same time five feet into air.

C. Allow orbiters to come down and loop one orbiter string with arm.

D. Allow string to loop around your wrist with other orbiter.

E. Flip upward five feet into air.

F. Catch handle or string near handle and bring arm over.

G. Start horizontal movements and achieve Horizontal Eskimo Orbit.

70. Horizontal Toss — Loop Wrist — Flip Vertical Eskimo Orbit

A. Hold Eskimo Yo-Yo as shown.

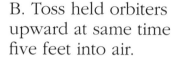

B. Toss held orbiters upward at same time five feet into air.

C. Allow orbiters to come down and loop one orbiter string with arm.

D. Allow string to loop around your wrist with other orbiter.

E. Flip upward five feet into air.

F. Catch handle or string near handle and start vertical movements.

G. Achieve Vertical Eskimo Orbit.

71. Horizontal Toss — 360 — Loop Wrist — Flip Horizontal Eskimo Orbit

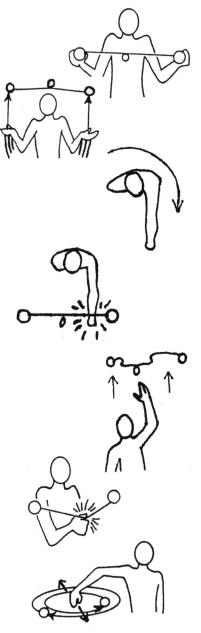

A. Hold Eskimo Yo-Yo as shown.

B. Toss held orbiters upward at same time several feet into air.

C. Turn in a complete circle quickly.

D. Allow orbiters to come down and loop one orbiter string with arm.

E. Flip upward five feet into air.

F. Catch handle or string near handle and bring arm over.

H. Start horizontal movements and achieve Horizontal Eskimo Orbit.

72. Horizontal Toss — 360 — Flip
Vertical Eskimo Orbit

A. Hold Eskimo Yo-Yo as shown.

B. Toss held orbiters upward at same time several feet into air.

C. Turn in a complete circle quickly.

D. Allow orbiters to come down and loop one orbiter string with arm.

E. Flip upward five feet into air.

F. Catch handle or string near handle.

G. Start vertical movements and achieve Vertical Eskimo Orbit.

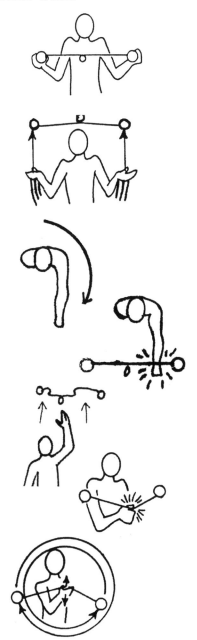

73. Single Floor Pickup — Toss
Vertical Eskimo Orbit

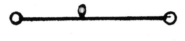

A. Place Eskimo Yo-Yo on floor as shown.

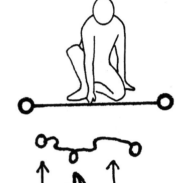

B. Stoop down to grasp handle.

C. Stand up quickly and toss Eskimo Yo-Yo up into air.

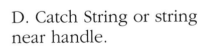

D. Catch String or string near handle.

E. Achieve Vertical Eskimo Orbit.

74. Loop Chair Leg Start — Two Orbiters
Horizontal Eskimo Orbit

A. Place orbiters around chair leg as shown.

B. Grasp handle of Eskimo Yo-Yo.

C. Pull back on handle and stand up quickly.

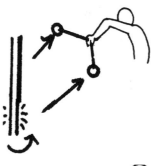

D. Start horizontal movements and achieve Horizontal Eskimo Orbit.

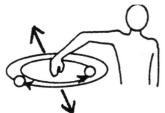

75. Two Hands — Behind The Back Toss Vertical Eskimo Orbit

A. Hold orbiters behind back with both hands as shown.

B. Toss orbiters upward over your head five feet.

C. Catch handle or string near handle and start vertical movements.

D. Achieve Vertical Eskimo Orbit.

76. Pickup Toss
Vertical Eskimo Orbit

A. Hold Eskimo Yo-Yo
as shown.

B. Toss Eskimo Yo-
Yo straight up into air
several feet.

C. Catch handle or
string near handle
and start vertical
movements.

D. Achieve Vertical
Eskimo Orbit.

77. Pickup Toss
Horizontal Eskimo Orbit

A. Hold both orbiters in one hand as shown.

B. Toss held orbiters upward several feet.

C. Catch handle or string near handle, bend arm over and start horizontal movements.

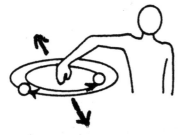

D. Achieve Horizontal Eskimo Orbit.

78. Pickup Toss — 360 Vertical Eskimo Orbit

A. Hold both orbiters in one hand as shown.

B. Toss held orbiters upward several feet.

C. Quickly turn in a circle.

D. Catch handle or string near handle and start vertical movements

E. Achieve Vertical Eskimo Orbit.

79. Horizontal Toss — 360 Horizontal Eskimo Orbit

A. Hold both orbiters in one hand as shown.

B. Toss held orbiters upward several feet.

C. Quickly turn in a circle.

D. Catch handle or string near handle and achieve Horizontal Eskimo Orbit.

80. Full Conversion — Overhead, Vertical, and Horizontal Eskimo Orbits

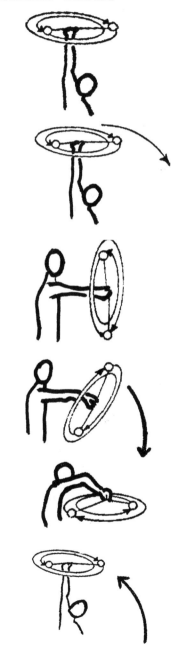

A. Achieve Overhead Eskimo Orbit.

B. Start bringing twirling orbiters downward.

C. Bring orbiters to Vertical Eskimo Orbit

D. Start bringing twirling orbiters downward.

E. Achieve Horizontal Eskimo Orbit.

F. Bring twirling orbiters back up to Overhead Eskimo Obit slowly.

81. Swing And Loop Around Wrist Vertical Eskimo Orbit

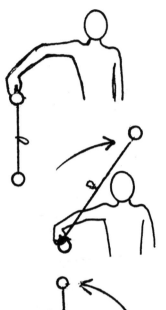

A. Hold Eskimo Yo-Yo as shown.

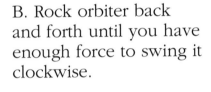

B. Rock orbiter back and forth until you have enough force to swing it clockwise.

C. Extend wrist out allowing orbiter string to wrap around and swing other orbiter in opposite direction.

D. Catch handle or string near handle as it swings around.

E. Achieve Vertical Eskimo Orbit.

82. Drop Orbiters — Loop Wrist — Twirl Vertical Eskimo Orbit

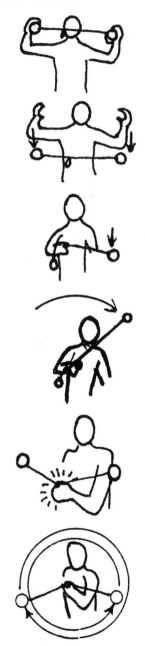

A. Hold orbiters in both hands as shown.

B. Drop orbiters at the same time.

C. Drop left hand down quickly allowing string to loop over it.

D. Allow string to swing around clockwise.

E. Catch handle or string near handle.

F. Achieve Vertical Eskimo Orbit.

83. Loop One Wrist — Flip
Vertical Eskimo Orbit

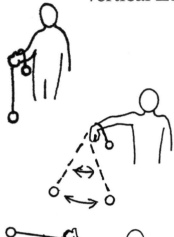

A. Put string over wrist as shown.

B. Rock back and forth until you can swing it around clockwise.

C. Move wrist quickly until you can flip Eskimo Yo-Yo several feet upward.

D. Catch handle or string near handle and start vertical movements.

E. Achieve Vertical Eskimo Orbit.

84. Orbiter Rock — Flip
Vertical Eskimo Orbit

A. Allow string to hang over index fingers.

B. Start rocking orbiters back and forth.

C. Quickly flip both orbiters upward several feet.

D. Catch handle or string near handle of Eskimo Yo-Yo.

E. Achieve Vertical Eskimo Orbit.

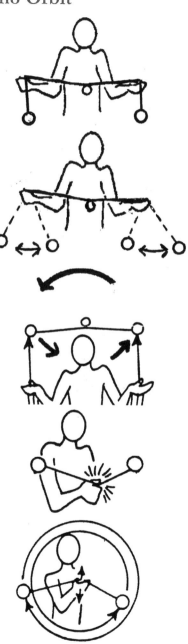

85. Twirl Around String — Toss Vertical Eskimo Orbit

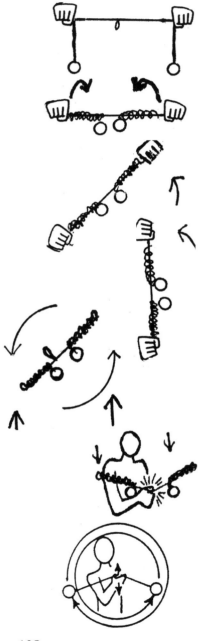

A. Hold sting in each hand as shown.

B. Start circular motion with both hands causing string to wrap around string.

C. Raise one arm upward in a slight motion.

D. Raising arm is now moving to vertical motion.

E. At this time, quickly release sting causing it to go upward in air.

F. Catch string or string near handle and start vertical movements.

G. String will unravel and you can now achieve Vertical Eskimo Orbit.

86. Twirl Around Pole Toss
Horizontal Eskimo Orbit

A. Stand for feet for a pole.

B. Hold Eskimo Yo-Yo as shown.

C. Put arm behind you and swing orbiter around and throw toward pole.

D. Allow string near end of orbiter to swing around on its own power.

E. Catch handle or string near handle of Eskimo Yo-Yo.

E. Achieve Horizontal Eskimo Orbit.

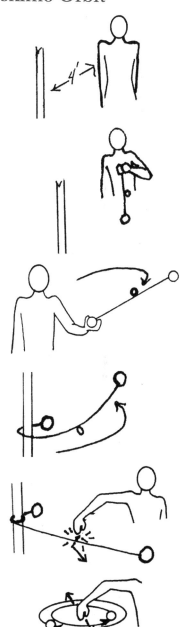

87. Loop The Finger — Reverse Direction Vertical Eskimo Orbit

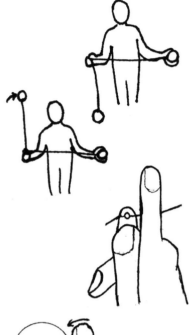

A. Hold handle and orbiter as shown.

B. Start twirling orbiter in clockwise.

C. Stick first index finger out while twirling orbiter.

D. Allow string to wind around index finger.

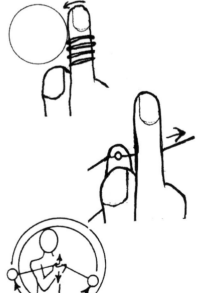

E. Start twirling orbiter in opposite direction until it is unwound.

F. Start vertical movements and achieve Vertical Eskimo Orbit.

88. One Hand - Behind The Back Toss — Vertical Eskimo Orbit

A. Hold both orbiters in one hand as shown.

B. Toss held orbiters upward.

C. Catch handle or string near handle.

D. Achieve Vertical Eskimo Orbit.

89. One hand — Behind The Back Toss Horizontal Eskimo Orbit

A. Hold both orbiters in one hand as shown.

B. Toss held orbiters upward.

C. Catch handle or string near handle and bring arm over.

D. Achieve Horizontal Eskimo Orbit.

90. Dead Start — Vertical and Overhead Eskimo Orbits

A. Hold Eskimo Yo-Yo as shown.

B. Start vertical jerking movement causing orbiters to move back and forth.

C. Achieve Vertical Eskimo Orbit.

D. Bring operating arm up slowly until achieving Overhead Eskimo Orbit.

E. Bring operating arm down slowly until achieving Vertical Eskimo Orbit.

113

91. Dead Start — Horizontal , Vertical, and Overhead Eskimo Orbits

A. Hold Eskimo Yo-Yo as shown.

B. Start horizontal jerking movements and achieve Eskimo Orbit.

C. Bring operating arm up slowly until achieving Vertical Eskimo Orbit.

D. Bring operating arm up slowly until achieving Overhead Eskimo Orbit.

92. 360 Overhead Eskimo — Orbit Hand Switch — Overhead Eskimo Orbits

A. Achieve Overhead Eskimo Orbit.

B. Start turning around slowly while continuing Overhead Eskimo Orbit.

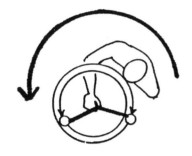

C. Switch operating hands at different times while continuing operation.

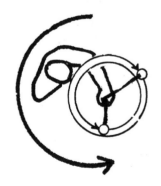

93. Pole Toss
Horizontal Eskimo Orbit

A. Achieve Horizontal Eskimo Orbit while standing four feet from a pole.

B. Take one step forward toward pole.

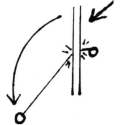

C. Toss Eskimo Yo-Yo when orbiters are directly behind you and time it so that one orbiter string wraps around pole.

D. Wait for swing orbiter to come around and catch string or string near handle.

E. Take one step back and achieve Horizontal Eskimo Orbit.

94. Pole Toss
Vertical Eskimo Orbit

A. Achieve Horizontal Eskimo Orbit while standing four feet from a pole.

B. Take one step forward toward pole.

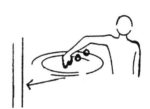

C. Toss Eskimo Yo-Yo when orbiters are directly behind you and time it so that one orbiter string wraps around pole.

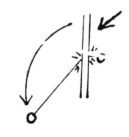

D. Wait for swing orbiter to come around and catch string or string near handle.

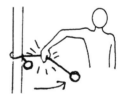

E. Achieve Vertical Eskimo Orbit.

95. Twirl Around Pole Toss
Vertical Eskimo Orbit

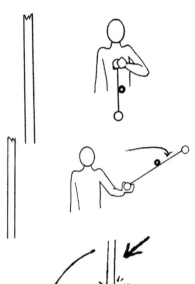

A. Stand four feet from a pole and hold Eskimo Yo-Yo as shown.

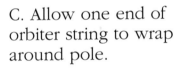

B. Twirl Eskimo Yo-Yo around toward vertical pole.

C. Allow one end of orbiter string to wrap around pole.

D. Catch swing orbiter handle or string near handle.

E. Achieve Vertical Eskimo Orbit.

96. Pendulum Rock Behind Back – Toss Vertical Eskimo Orbit

A. Hold orbiter in one hand behind back as shown.

B. Start rocking orbiter back and forth.

C. Toss into air behind your back allowing orbiters to go upward.

D. Turn around to catch the handle or string near handle.

E. Achieve Vertical Eskimo Orbit.

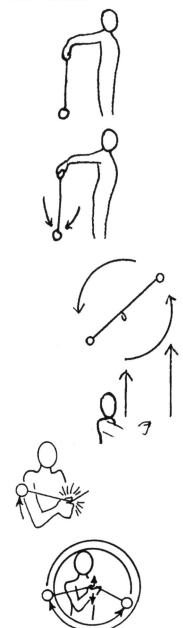

97. Jack Knife – Reverse Directions Vertical Eskimo Orbit

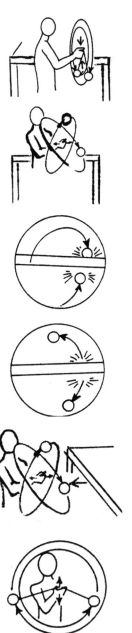

A. Achieve Vertical Eskimo Orbit standing three feet from a tabletop.

B. Achieve Jack Knife and prepare to move horizontally toward, moving when orbiters are both behind you.

C. Move operating arm toward tabletop.

D. Allow orbiters to hit top and bottom of table.

E. Move operating arm outward away from table and achieve Jack knife movements.

E. Switch to vertical movements and achieve Vertical Eskimo Orbit.

98. Double Floor Pickup
Double Vertical Eskimo Orbit

A. Place Eskimo Yo-Yo either sideways or toward front and back on floor.

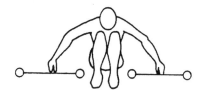

B. Stand up quickly and start vertical movements of Eskimo Yo-Yo.

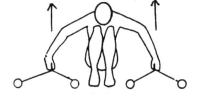

C. Achieve Double Vertical Eskimo Yo-Yo.

99. Double Floor Pickup
Double Horizontal Eskimo Orbits

A. Place Eskimo Yo-Yos on floor as shown and grasp handles.

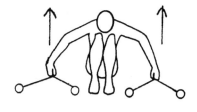

B. Prepare to stand up and twirl Eskimo Yo-Yos.

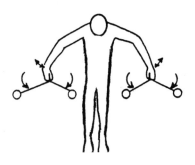

C. Stand up quickly and start horizontal movements of Eskimo Yo-Yos.

D. Achieve Double Horizontal Eskimo Orbits.

100. Double Dead Starts
Double Vertical Eskimo Orbits

A. Hold two sets of Eskimo Yo-Yos ash shown.

B. Start up and down jerking movements of both Eskimo Yo-Yos.

C. Achieve Double Eskimo Orbits.

History of Tricks Mastered

Not everyone will be able to master all of the 100 tricks: only the few and the brave will even try. If you're one of the few and the brave who master all 100 tricks, send your information, and Chris will send you a beautiful certificate, suitable for framing, confirming that you have mastered all 100 tricks. To receive your beautiful *Alaska Eskimo Yo-Yo Master Certificate*, master all 100 tricks, have a witness sign and date the *History of Tricks Mastered* form, and send the following information:

Name _____

Address_____

City _____ **State** _____ **Zip** _____

Email Address _____

Send your information to:
Publication Consultants
PO Box 221974
Anchorage, Alaska 99528
Fax: (907) 349-2424
Email: books@publicationconsultants.com

Trick	Witness	Date	Page
1.			24
2.			25
3.			26
4.			27
5.			28

Trick	Witness	Date	Page
6.			29
7.			30
8.			31
9.			32
10.			33
11.			34
12.			35
13.			36
14.			37
15.			38
16.			39
17.			40
18.			41
19.			42
20.			43
21.			44
22.			45
23.			46
24.			47
25.			48
26.			49
27.			50
28.			51
29.			52

Trick	Witness	Date	Page
30.			53
31.			54
32.			55
33.			56
34.			57
35.			58
36.			59
37.			60
38.			61
39.			62
40.			63
41.			64
42.			65
43.			66
44.			67
45.			68
46.			69
47.			70
48.			71
49.			72
50.			73
51.			74
52.			75
53.			76

Trick	Witness	Date	Page
54. _____			77
55. _____			78
56. _____			79
57. _____			80
58. _____			81
59. _____			82
60. _____			83
61. _____			84
62. _____			85
63. _____			86
64. _____			87
65. _____			88
66. _____			89
67. _____			90
68. _____			91
69. _____			92
70. _____			93
71. _____			94
72. _____			95
73. _____			96
74. _____			97
75. _____			98
76. _____			99
77. _____			100

Trick	Witness	Date	Page
78. _____			101
79. _____			102
80. _____			103
81. _____			104
82. _____			105
83. _____			106
84. _____			107
85. _____			108
86. _____			109
87. _____			110
88. _____			111
89. _____			112
90. _____			113
91. _____			114
92 _____			115
93. _____			116
94. _____			117
95. _____			118
96. _____			119
97. _____			120
98. _____			121
99. _____			122
100. _____			123

Made in the USA
Charleston, SC
17 October 2011